i

c

o

p

e

Typesetting by Julia Natt
Cover Design by Peter Campanelli
ISBN - 978-1-948700-10-8

THE ACCOMPLICES:
A Civil Coping Mechanisms Book

For more information, find CCM at:

http://copingmechanisms.net

TOM
SAWYER

POEMS

JOSEPH GRANTHAM

for mom, dad, and mik

It being strictly the history of a boy, it must stop here;
the story could not go much further without becoming
the history of a man.
– Mark Twain, *The Adventures of Tom Sawyer*

You're so old
You must be 23
- "Crazy," Galaxie 500

life poem

stuff suddenly happens
stuff keeps happening
stuff stops happening

this existence

most of the time
i am
bored and warm

bus poem

the bus driver missed a turn
he was lost
he needed
directions
so we sat
and waited for him
to receive
directions
from a human voice
detached from the human
and funneled through a radio
a passenger from the back
came forward
and said
why aren't we moving
and the driver said
because i am lost

boo hoo

i don't think
living life
is all that
great
and i don't have to
i didn't ask to be here
but now i'm here
and i'm afraid of death
something i didn't know existed
before i existed
anyway retail sucks
and that's what i do
with most of my hours
and it's draining
makes you feel hopeless
makes you feel worthless
makes you feel like life is about paychecks that come
once every two weeks
and aren't enough
but maybe this is what being alive is all about
not having enough
having some of enough
a little bit of enough
i have to tell you though
asking someone for money
is never fun
and no
i don't want anymore
peanut butter toast

sad poem

we live in a world
where i write poems
about one person
who made me sad
a long time ago

work poem

it takes all day
for most people to decide
whether or not
they want a bag
i don't know what kind
of person you are
but i am
a shoes in the house
kind of guy
i never take them off

poem for jessie

my friend jessie
hates poems
about sex

but mitch
(a man i barely know)
asked me

your writing is
primarily
about sex
right?

and he was wrong

but this poem is

i think i was
choked last night
during sexual intercourse
but i can't remember
and i don't know why
what if she
was choking me
because she was bored
because i was annoying
because i was bart simpson
because i was ugly
and she wanted to see
what it would look like
to have a dead boy
in her bed
who could blame her

ask me anything

at bars
bartenders ask
what's the name on your card
and i say
grantham
and they look confused
so i say
joseph
and they look confused
so i say
joseph grantham
and they bring me back
my card
and to life
and i give them a tip

at panera bread
they ask
chips apple or baguette
and i say *apple*
but i always throw the apple
away
or at someone

at grocery stores
they ask
did you find everything all right
and i say
everything wasn't all right
but yes
i found everything

love poem

i love pickles
and you
you love pickles
and not me

things she told me on the phone

she told me
when i think
of you
i think
of the color
maroon
i thought
but i am
blue
a dark blue

she told me
you've got
a kansas city accent
but only when you talk
on the phone
i thought
maybe my father
is to blame
but i lived there
for two years
when i was ages
one and two
maybe being born there
forever gave me
a kansas city accent

she told me
you need to stop
calling me
or maybe i just heard that
in her voice

dad poem

i have a father
he is my dad
he grew up
in kansas city

he was born
on the same street
as charlie parker
but it was a long street

he had a friend
called tuna
tuna shot hoops
and always played quarterback
in the pick-up games
tuna was a success
with the ladies
when i met tuna
he was an older tuna
but he was still shooting hoops

the sound of my father's voice
is midwestern
and did you know that he has a small notebook
in which he records
the amount of dollars
and cents
he spends
on a tank of gas
each time

he fills
his car
he has filled
multiple notebooks
with this information
do you have a father
who does this too?

one more thing

when i am trying
to sound personable
i put on
the voice
of my father
and it always works

poem for derick

derick stand next to me
the color of your shirt
brings out something special
in my eyes
but also derick
there's something
you must know
you have one of the worst names
a person could have

good body

the kid in our neighborhood
with the good body
he went missing

he had a body that could breathe
and a body that could run and do push-ups
but we always knew he'd go missing

and when they found him
he was all sorts of beaten up and bloody
but he was wearing his favorite shirt
and we said

look at that

would you look at that

that's a great t shirt

no i didn't

i got a job
one summer
working for
famous amos cookies
no i didn't

slow poem

people are so slow
in new york city
so you have to
kill them
and climb over
their dead bodies
to get
where you're going
but you better hope
no one thinks
you're slow
today i was walking
behind a man
who sneezed
with every step
and then he hocked
and spit
into the dirt
next to a tree
and when i passed
by the glob
it shined in the sun
like a diamond
or a piece
of broken glass
and i wanted
to pick it up

fat poem

i've been thinking
about a lot of stuff
too much stuff
fills my skull
my whole body
and i am tired
of the stuff
sometimes i write it down
sometimes i read it
i mostly sit
and eat it
and corpulence
maybe it's not such a bad thing
or a bad idea
to become
fat
a fat guy
a big fat guy

urology poem

in the basement
waiting to find out
if i have
cancer
or something
like it

a woman nearby
with an amputated leg
waggles her stump
she's on the phone

one thing
led to another
gangrenous
had to go

she seems
well-adjusted
to her phantom limb

the purpose of life is to die

the purpose of life
is to die
peacefully
in your sleep
but i had a scare
in november 2016
i found blood
in my piss
and in my cum
when i came
into a ball
of toilet paper
that was strange
telling my father
and my doctor
hey dad
hey doc
i found blood
in my urine
and in my semen
and the doc
checked my prostate
which is a euphemism
for saying
he stuck his finger
up my ass
i'd been afraid
of that moment
for years
more afraid of it

than cancer itself
and then it happened
so fast
and it was fine
of course it was fine
then doc asked
if i'd been having
rough sex
but i hadn't been
having sex
with anyone
other than myself
and when the blood work
came back
he said i was fine
and that i could do
a lot more damage
to myself
while i was still
in my twenties
so now i drink
most nights
and smoke cigarettes
when i can
and make a habit
of eating pizza
and ice cream
because
i am still
in my twenties

good news

i am pretty sure
the day after i die
someone will email me
with good news
about something

work poem

i always eat lunch
in the laundromat
and i'm always on my way
to the thing
where i sit in the bathroom
in the dark
for eight hours
and get a paycheck
two weeks later
tonight's customer complimented
my mustache
and i wanted to tell him
what the bus driver told me
information gladly given but
safety requires avoiding
unnecessary conversation

happy poem

twinkle twinkle
little poem
i am me
and i hope i don't die
in a car crash
or in an anything
i want to live forever
even when i am sad
i want to be happy
i will try
to keep going
at least
as long as
mom and dad
are still alive

it won't take long

have bad
sex
with me

god i want these things

i wish i liked
more than one song
by
camper van beethoven
but other than that skinhead song
i've got nothing
i wish other songs
by
stereolab
made me feel the way
'lo boob oscillator'
does
but they don't
i know there's someone
somewhere
saying
but they have so many good songs
but that's not what this is about
there's always someone
somewhere
saying something
and have you seen
high fidelity
when i was young
i wanted to be john cusack
in that movie
i wanted to be an asshole
but i turned out nice
although
i'm sure i can find someone
who thinks
i'm a dick

work poem

another sunday
another old white man
buying biographies
of adolf hitler
another stranger
asking me where
the restroom is
located
it's behind the travel section
you need a quarter
to unlock the door

poem for billy

last night
at work
while we moved chairs
billy told me all
about robert altman

i know some things
about robert altman

i know a thing or two
about robert altman

but billy told me things
i didn't know
about robert altman

but
the thing is
billy also told me
things i know
about robert altman

poem for no one in particular

you were my
soulmate
i know i know
that's a funny word
you threw me
for a loop
and
off a cliff
i understand that
i hated you
for the first few seconds
but i was falling
for so long
that i fell in love with you
again
right before
i hit the ground

breakfast poem

this morning
everyone
on the train
was snorting up phlegm
and swallowing it

work poem

sometimes all you can do
is pretend you don't
understand someone
and the thought of
money
scares me
less
than the thought of
no money
while i was writing this
an italian baby
stared at me
from his place
in the arms
of his father
and i thought
one day
that boy
will read
the adventures of
tom sawyer

poem for mik

a good sister
teaches her brother
how to scrape plaque
off of his teeth
with a paperclip

a bad sister
throws a bottle of
nail polish remover
at her brother's head

certain places

sometimes i wonder
if certain places
(like the dark corner
in an albertson's
where they store the canned soda)
wish they were different places

work poem

think about the floor
where you work
is it
hardwood
cement
dirt
tile
carpet
is it cold
somehow warm
why don't you ever think
about the floor
at your place
of work

i hear a stranger
talking about a funeral
on the phone
on the train
on my way to work
and i want to go
to that funeral
because
i've never been
to a funeral
and
because
i don't want to go
to work

name poem

sometimes my sister's name
is mikaela
other times
it is mik
in the early nineties
it was a popular choice
for a name

my mother's name
is patricia
but she goes by patti
don't you dare
call her patricia

my grandfather changed
his name
from miles
to joe
and now that is
my father's name
and my name too

but everyone who knows me
calls me joey

everyone who likes me
calls me joey

everyone who hates me
calls me joey

everyone who feels nothing about me
calls me joey

you can
call me joey

haircut poem

almost cut my hair
it happened just the other day
i was trying to impress someone
who no longer looks at me
who no longer thinks about me
who thinks about me?
i wonder
and i wander too
but usually just down the street
to get a snack
so tomorrow morning
i'll eat graham crackers
and coffee
for breakfast

mega poem

i take the bus
to go see her
because she's not there

silver beach

i was living on an island
called shelter island
i found a shell
on a beach
on the island
and i brought it back
to her
in the city
which was also
an island
her own island
they call that one
manhattan
i looped a string
through the shell
so the shell
became a necklace
and when i gave it to her
she thought it was
dumb
but i think she still has it
maybe she threw it away
how would i know
i would have to ask her
and i am afraid
of what she might say
and sometimes
i am afraid
of what i might do
one day

septucation

last night i heard the word
septucation
in my head
it's not a word
or i thought i saw it in a book
i don't smell good
i read the other day
in a newspaper
that a man was decreased

work poem

it's sunday
so that means
i'm hungover
at work again
but i like this
feeling
feels like
i'm hiding
under a blanket
except that
everyone can see me
and i don't have
any language
anymore
but here are your books
you bought them
take them home
do what you will

poem for richard simmons

richard simmons
was born
in new orleans

i thought he was from
new york
maybe
los angeles

richard simmons
is from
new orleans

oh
and his name is
milton

artificial love poem

what's her name?
what does she look like?
i'm not gonna say
i'm not sure
i'm gonna buy it now
i'm not gonna say it to me
i'm sure that it will not work

poem for bud smith

you work a lot harder
than me
and almost everyone
i know
you work harder
than i'll ever work
in my entire life
thank you
for not making me
feel bad
for going to college
thank you
for letting me crash
on your coleman air mattress
thank you
for showing me
jersey
thank you
for making happiness
look cool
i am so sick
of being sad

anhedonia

one of my favorite words is
anhedonia
because it sounds like a place
a faraway place
a made-up place
a place from a bad novel
but really
the word describes
an inability
or an unwillingness
to feel pleasure
and really
you could have
looked it up
if you didn't already know that

parent poem

i'm so sad
about the death
of my parents
but they haven't
died
yet
and as far
as we know
they never will

work poem

i was on my
lunch break
at panucho's
and i saw someone
who looked like you
she was eating a churro
it seemed like something
you would do
later a man with a small mouth
asked me about a business book
i flossed my teeth yesterday
on your couch
while your friend
mopped the floor
around us
we couldn't go anywhere
until the floor dried

bad date

i am going to tell
the one
about the bad date

i've been telling that one
for so long
for years

she said i was
her type
a soft bookseller
not a soft hotel

she made me kiss her
even though she was sick
and after the kisses
i was scared
i was going to get sick

and last night
i drank the tea
straight from the teddy bear
and i told this same damn story
again

good date

stomach hurt
from eating
carrots all day
at work
but when i got to the bar
it settled
drank two red stripes
she drank one
she had a seltzer too
talked about growing up
catholic
confession
never telling the priest
when we masturbated
or when we
did anything
she was much more beautiful
than i was
and smarter too
i think
and at the end of the date
we hugged a couple times
and went our separate ways

poem a date might write about me

his mustache tasted of beer
and food
and breath
his chin wasn't receding
but his jaw wasn't strong
there's always something
wrong
with the men i meet at bars
he couldn't keep the lenses
of his glasses clean
he didn't talk
and then he talked too much
and when he smiled
his face got fatter
every once in a while
he looked
and seemed
okay though

honey poem

i don't think i've ever dated
an american playwright
i don't think i've ever dated
an american anything
one time i had a girlfriend
who wouldn't let me call her
my girlfriend
she made me call her
my honey
which always felt
strange
but sometimes
i still miss
my honey

creek poem

i've never painted a fence
fuck fences
there was a hole in one
we crawled through
franny dropped her jeans
and peed right there
in the creek
and then we took our shovels
and tried to dig a hole
to china
or wherever it is
people dig holes to
but then we had to go home
because jack's mom (karen) was upset
she didn't like how we ruined
jack's jack-o-lantern
and left pumpkin
all over her garage

work poem

i've never done anything
that wasn't amazing
except there were some breakfasts
that were boring
but i probably saved the lives
of your children
if you lived in dublin, california
between the years of
1993-1995
when i served as lifeguard
of the briarhill swimming pool

poem for scott mcclanahan

my favorite writer
taught me
how to hit
myself
in the face
he didn't know
he was teaching me
that
he didn't know
me
but
he does now
he wrote a scene
in a novel
where he hit
himself
in the face
and then
i started
doing
the same thing

important poem

it's important
that you
climb trees

and it's important
that you are
important

it's important
that you
brush your hair
and your teeth
at the same time

it's also important
that you make
less money
than your coworkers

and it's important
that you complain

it's important
that you drink coffee
all day long

and it's important
that you are tired
when you get home
and when you die

it's important
that you do the things
you want to do
before you don't

juvenile poem

when i was a kid
and i still am one
my unborn children
lived and died
in socks
underneath my bed

when i was a kid
and i still am one
i wanted to be everything
astronaut/actor/reader/writer
all in one

but then i found out
i was afraid
of outer space
and what it could do
to your body
and i was afraid
of people
and what they could do
to your body

mom poem

i think about my mom
growing up
in tarzana
in the valley
in the southern part of the state of california
and how once she was locked in a dark closet
by her brothers
loren/eric
and how once she was swept away by the sea
on a raft
with her friend
melinda
she probably never thought
one day i'll have a boy
who will want to die

but there are good things too
like when i was growing up
she would go on business trips
and before she left
early in the morning
i would hear her suitcase
rolling along
the tile floor of the kitchen
toward the front door
and i would yell
from my bed
mom!
and she would yell
yeah honey?

and i would yell
i love you!
and she would walk
back to my bedroom
to see my face
to kiss my forehead
and to tell me
she loved me too

work poem

i fought fires
for a few years
before i became
an actor
and when i was
an actor
i was typecast
as a firefighter
and i fought
fake fires
until i quit
acting altogether
and became a bagger
at a grocery store
around the corner
from my apartment
and then i became
a hero
and employee of the month
while i was a bagger
when i stopped
a man with a gun
from holding us up
by hitting him
on his head
with a can
of soup

poem for mr. popovich

in p.e. class
we had to run a mile
once a year
and i was scared of that
and i didn't know if i could do it
and i had more weight
than some of the other kids
we all had more weight maybe
we were all fat maybe
we were growing
into ourselves
or that's what we were told
and that's what we then told ourselves
to make ourselves feel better
about ourselves
but i remember thinking
while running
and panting
and wanting it to end
that mr. popovich should run too
he should run with us
if he is the p.e. teacher
he should show us
that he can run a mile too

overheard construction worker on subway platform

she'd go see this other guy
for a while
and then she found out
what he really was
and she'd come back
she would break up with me
and she would come back
she would break up with me
and she would come back
other guys would be licking
their tongues
she had a kid
i never met her kid
oh my god
she was a lot of fun to be with
i kept trying to get dates
she was 35
oh my god
and when she drank
she got even more
friendlier

poem for charlie chaplin

charlie chaplin died
on christmas
in 1977

charlie chaplin was born
four days before adolf hitler
in the year 1889

and they both had that fucking mustache
but charlie chaplin was older
so it's his mustache

valentino's market

my wife is standing
close behind me
in line
at the grocery store
except that
i'm twenty-three years old
and i don't have a wife
she's just the first person
to stand this close to me
in a long time
and my only plans
tonight and in this life
are to make a pot
of lentil soup

poem for grandma

grandma got in trouble
for smoking cigarettes
grandma sent me two hundred
dollars every two months
when i was in college
grandma wants me
to get a girlfriend
and so does america
i'll see what i can do
i've been using
the dandruff shampoo
as body wash
for the past month
because i didn't feel
like buying a bar
of soap

bus poem

tonight
i heard
an ambulance stutter
and the woman
sitting in front of me
her hair
draped over her seat
tickled my knees

airport poem

old people reading
spy/mystery novels
have old bodies

but in their minds
they are jumping
over things
and solving crimes
and shooting stuff

know it all

a lot of life
is like
someone
approaching you
tapping you
on the shoulder
to tell you
that the skin
is the largest organ
of the human body
and you
have to say
yes
yes i know that
most people know that
by now
you're not special
but thank you
anyway

namesake

funny story
think it might be true
the first police constable
in the united kingdom
to be killed
while on duty
was named
joseph grantham
and hey
that's my name too

in 1830
he was kicked
in the temple
by two drunkards
blunt trauma

poem for sam #1

i have a couple of friends
named sam
most people do
one of them said
sex smells like
bad honey
he's the one i met
in a high school
weight training class
the first time we hung out
outside of class
we went to see
an iranian film
about divorce
at a theater called
the dome

poem for sam #2

sam messaged me
stop filming yourself
hitting yourself
and posting it
on the internet
you are freaking
me out
lol

then
over eggs
over medium
sam said
it just seems like
you are trying
to get revenge
like you want her
to see you
hitting yourself
like you want her
to worry about you
and feel sad

and damn it
if sam
wasn't right

angry new york poem

if you're from new york
then you don't what it's like to live

in new york

ridgewood

trying to masturbate
but i can hear
my roommate
playing youtube videos
of video game walkthroughs
in the other room
and i want to see
if i can put my head
through a cement wall
and i want to see
if i can feel myself die

poem for nick

nick sold me
his sister's old phone
for fifty dollars

i was poor
but i needed
a phone
we all do
so i bought it

i spend my life
charging
this phone

it always dies
when i need it
most

you're a good friend but
fuck you nick

you can't have everything

i don't have
a friend
named bruce

subway poem

standing by the tracks
i have the urge
to shadowbox
in public
and scream
at the top of my mother
fucking lungs

poem for charles bukowski

i hate people who say
i hate charles bukowski
and i hate people who say
i will hunt down
each and every one
of your family members
and kill them
one by one
i hate people who say that
i also hate people who say
i love charles bukowski
because they're too happy
about it
they're smiling
like they just got away
with something
something like
kicking their wife
off of the couch
eating a payday
candy bar meal
or killing
an entire bottle
of alcohol
any kind

dream poem

i had a dream last night
hang on
the dream was only one sentence long

a celebrity walking through the city
recognized a homeless man
from all of her favorite
alleys and subway stops

see
that wasn't so bad

newspaper

in the morning
i read
between the crimes

confession poem

i need to get
something
from the store

and off of my chest

here it is

for as long as i
can remember

i have been alive

i have committed
the sin
of immortality

and i am sorry

boring poem

it's awesome
how boring
life is
like today
i was in a supermarket
and i saw
all of the carrots
and i wished
i worked
in the supermarket
and i saw
an old lady
her body
hunched over
reaching for oranges
and she looked like this letter

F

and i wanted to offer
to help her
but i knew if i did
i'd be helping her
my whole life

poem for leonard michaels

my favorite writer was dead so i dug up his bones
and brought them to a party

can we smoke in here, the bones asked
and i told the bones, *you could probably get away with
anything in here*

how does he do it, the guests asked, *how does he move and
breathe and smoke*

he is my favorite writer, i told them
was, the bones said

how many of those do you have, the guests asked
how many whats, i said
favorite writers, they said
lots, i said

how did this one die, they wanted to know

he died during surgery on his colon, i told them
the papers reported complications from bowel surgery, the
bones added

everyone laughed
fecal matter was funny
bowel was an intimate word

at the end of the night i returned to the graveyard with the
bones
and put them back in the ground

it was a good night, i told the bones
goodnight, the bones said

current mood

coffee
rolling chair

egg breakfast
ejaculation

dancing in front of
the bathroom mirror
wearing my
stained
six color
favorite shirt

and nothing else

movement

i place my thigh
upon my thigh
it's easy to do

home poem

i don't have any special skills
and if i did
i wouldn't want them
i want to make 12 dollars an hour
or less
for the rest of my life
i want to live at home
with my parents
and with a fisher price castle
and some action figures
that way i can close the door
to my bedroom
and use the hasbro
to make stories happen

dream poem

thomas pynchon cormac mccarthy and j.d. salinger
live in an apartment in a city

they eat meals together and think about things
they talk about them too

but then one day j.d. breaks his hip
and it all goes downhill

he dies a painless death and
pynchon and mccarthy mourn
the loss of their roommate

by drinking a few cold ones
and performing their secret handshake

physical

you look like a young picasso, my doctor told me
it's all in the nose, he said
my legs dangled off of the table
picasso had a big nose, he said

oh no poem

oh no
i was on my way to a party
i almost got hit by a car
i am always almost getting hit by cars
i said that out loud
i said
i am always almost getting hit by cars
and i thought that was funny
so i wrote it down
before i got to the party
because i started carrying around a moleskine journal
because maybe i have become 'that guy'
oh no

poem for anton yelchin

this morning
i read
about the actor's death
in bed
on the toilet
crushed by a car
i walked
stepped
on a snake
it got away
in the road
i saw a squirrel
brain
crushed by a car
thought
that's kinda like
the other thing
the thing i read about
this morning

place poem

you'll never be
in front of yourself
or behind yourself
or to the left of yourself
or to the right of yourself
you'll always be
where you are

poem for philip k dick

philip k dick was born
in 1928
he died
in 1982

i think it's cool
that when you reverse
the 28
you get
82
and i don't know why
but
it seems fitting
for him

but also maybe
i've just had
too much coffee

work poem

it sucks that
to come into an inheritance
people have to die
today i put almonds
in my pocket
but there were coins
and bills in there too
so i threw it all away
lately i've been trying hard
to become
less annoying
less nice
kinder
to the people i hate
cruel
to the ones i love
we'll see
how it all goes

psa poem

the person behind this poem
has a beating heart
he is alive
and he doesn't really do any drugs
but it's only because he's scared
of almost everything
and has been for a long time
his whole life
and he's surprised you're here
and he doesn't really know how to tell you
that he is interesting
but he wants to make it clear
that he is interesting maybe
or maybe
he is boring
but above all
he knows how to scream

poem for dog

last night
i cried
and listened to
lucinda williams
i had a dog
named lucinda
she died of cancer
i saw it happen
and it's not fair
how often i talk
about suicide
it's like i'm trying
to usurp
the pain
of others
so let's talk about something else
i like that movie
bend it like beckham
it's funny
i haven't seen it
in a while
but i remember
being young
and i remember
laughing

show and tell

andrew showed us his dad
and told us his dad
was an orthopedic surgeon
so i asked him
whether or not
cracking my knuckles
would give me arthritis
and he paced around
the yellow tiles
of the church hall
and said something
in a professional tone
about how
the evidence is inconclusive
and
crack away

onomatopoeia poem

my dad had a tie rack
in his closet
he would press a button
and it would light up
and the ties would rotate
around an oval
and the machine
would make a whirring sound
that i can't express
with onomatopoeia
but that sound
is good
and that sound
is my childhood

pony poem

i think i am what
you'd call a sucker
because i pay for the bus
and i use cash and coins
and this group of guys
(all wearing sunglasses)
laughed at me
and then two stops later
the cops boarded the bus
and checked to see
who paid and who didn't
and the group of guys got kicked
off of the bus and fined
but now that i think about it
they may have just been laughing
at the way i look
because i look kind of funny
and today is my dad's 60th birthday
and also the kentucky derby
and my dad's horse didn't win
but i saw a pony
across the street from where i work
and i'm going to buy it for my mother

old poem

old people
love old
movies
and that
makes
perfect sense

thing i noticed

the word
imperceptibly
is almost always
preceded
by the word
almost
almost imperceptibly
maybe a lot of people notice
this
but for a while
i felt special
for noticing

work poem

my confidence
is directly proportional
to how strong
my jawline is
at any given
moment
so right now
i'd say
i'm not very confident
because i saw myself in a mirror
and it didn't look good
and because i ate a cookie
for lunch
and i'm in the self-help section
but only because i work here

blind poem

i went to
a retina specialist
to make sure
i wasn't
blind
i'm not blind but
i swear to god
for a minute there
i forgot
my eyeballs
are actual balls
full of jelly
they call that jelly
the vitreous humor
isn't that funny
and i guess
i am just a guy
who has floaters
in his humor

new poem

if this new poem
makes any sense
then i have failed you

the man was thirty
and he was thirsty
so he went into the kitchen

he grabbed a glass from the cabinet
above the sink
and he filled the glass with water

he drank the water
standing
leaning against the kitchen counter

that was just one moment
that happened in his life
and then he died forty-five years later

poem for centaurs

when i was younger
i looked at myself
naked in the mirror
and thought about my ass
and how it made me look
like a centaur

three haiku

the months are people
and every year we kill
all twelve of them, right?

and so we are all
serial killers killing
time just by living

maybe we should stop
give it a rest call it quits
it's gone on too long

novel poem

i wrote a novel
a couple years ago
that i never actually wrote
and no one published it
and no one read it
and for a while
i was really sad
about all of that
and so i never wrote the novel

poem for tony

tony is my only friend
who never existed
he died
he joined the army
he fought in a war
the war was fought
for oil and money
two of tony's favorite things
he just liked the way
they smelled
he died on a beach
thousands of miles away
from oil and money
a bullet in his stomach
but he didn't eat it
he was bleeding
he was happy
it felt good to know
that he could die

better off than some

on the bus
listening to the album
about the guy
who lost his wife
to cancer
she died
of cancer
he doesn't have her
anymore
and i thought i had
it bad
but
truth is
i am this close
to pissing in my pants
and every time the bus
hits a pothole
my bladder shrugs

commute poem

it's a good day
and a good sign
when the woman
next to you
on the train
coughs and coughs
her mouth open wide
while she stares into your eyes
and it's a good day
and a good sign
when the man
across from you
on the train
lights a cigarette
and proceeds to enjoy it
for the entirety of your commute
exhaling
hotboxing the subway car
with tobacco companies
don't change cars
stay on this one
this one is for you

travel guide

how far is it
to the nearest
death

poem for layla

sometimes i go on walks
and sometimes i don't
sometimes i sit around all day
that's okay
it's nice to have the option
last night i talked to the waitress
at the red bar
and her name was layla
today her name
is probably still layla
but you never know

fire hydrant

i stand on the sidewalk
i am done eating
fish and chips
i stare into a parking lot
my mom is in a building
behind me
buying me a cellphone
i'm still on
my parents' plan

work poem

i don't want to learn anything new
it's important that i think
i quit my job
i was shelving books again
derick i'm sorry
about what i said
about your name
you're a good guy
and maybe even
a bad person

poem for jersey city

i live in jersey city now
it's a thing that happens
when i am sad
and want to be happy
recommendation
don't do the in love falling thing
or do
i threw away a lot of stuff today
that ceramic cup you made
and that 'iowa dancers' t shirt you gave me
now i'm on the coleman air mattress
outside the window
i can hear
two voices
attached to people
talking about
the violence of dogs
and i can hear
the voices of dogs
attached to dog bodies
they have a lot to say
and the voices of cars
attached to car bodies
they have a lot to say too

life poem

i entered
i existed
i exited

ABOUT THE AUTHOR

JOSEPH GRANTHAM was born in Kansas City, Missouri.
He grew up in California. He read books for a while and
wrote bad stories and poems and went to school. Not much
happened. He lost his virginity when he was 18. He got
his BA from Bennington College. He still reads books and
writes. He runs Disorder Press with his sister.

OFFICIAL

CCM

GET OUT OF JAIL
* VOUCHER *

- -

Tear this out.

Skip that social event.

It's okay.

You don't have to go if you don't want to. Pick up
the book you just bought. Open to the first page.

You'll thank us by the third paragraph.

If friends ask why you were a no-show, show them

this voucher.

You'll be fine.

- -

We're coping.

CPSIA information can be obtained
at www.ICGtesting.com
Printed in the USA
BVHW07s0810221018
530870BV00009B/1119/P